The Awakening of Your Soul

The Awakening of Your Soul

A Collection of Poems

Latifah A. Hameen

Copyright © 2008 by Latifah A. Hameen.

ISBN: Softcover   978-1-4363-7800-0

All rights reserved. No part of this book may be reproduced or transmitted in any form or by any means, electronic or mechanical, including photocopying, recording, or by any information storage and retrieval system, without permission in writing from the copyright owner.

This book was printed in the United States of America.

To order additional copies of this book, contact:
Xlibris Corporation
1-888-795-4274
www.Xlibris.com
Orders@Xlibris.com

Contents

Mother Dear 11
My Father 12
My First Born Son 13
A Mother's Words Of Love 15
Finding Me 16
Kindness 17
When I Look In The Mirror 18
Perception Is Your Reality 19
Your Spirit 20
Live Your Dreams 21
Inside Of Me 22
Mothers, Let Me Say A Few Words 23
Phenomenal Woman 24
Failure Is Not Failure Until 26
God Grant Us Serenity 27
Creation 28
Prayer 29
The Believers 30
Our Black Brothers Struggle 31
In Waiting 32
That Illusion Of Being Black 33
A Better Me 35
Why Do I Feel Alienated 36
The Stranger Within 37
Wearing A Mask 39
Sistahs 41
Free To Be Me! 43
True Love 44
What Is Respect? 45
Look At Me! 46
Attitude 47
Depression Doesn't Live Here Anymore 49
Life For Me Ain't Been No Golden Stair 50

Tough Times	51
Why Me?	52
Self Love	54
I Am The One	55
The Best Is Yet To Come	56
The Real You	58
A Healthy Self-esteem	60
Existence	61
You Can Be The Star Of Your Show	62
Positive Attitude Seeds	63
The Human Being	64

With The Name of God, Most Gracious, Most Merciful

Dedication of this book

The Awakening of Your Soul is poetry that has been complied over years from either my direct experiences, or people and things that are near and dear to my heart. These poems are dedicated to all who are in constant search of truth, self-love and maintaining an inner peace of mind. I am continuously elevating to a higher spiritual level as I open my soul of expression through poetry and give to all who will embrace it, which in turn, I hope illuminates and sparks an interest of self-expression too. Whatever that expression looks like, let it be meaningful so it can touch and help others along the same path. I pray these poems will be inspiring, empowering and uplifting.

FOREWORD

**By
Talibah Mateen-Hooper
A Good Friend for 28 years**

WHEN I FIRST met Latifah Hameen back in 1980, we were both in college trying to get an education and make a difference in our lives. I found her to be a very funny and outgoing individual who always had a kind word whenever I was feeling sad.

Latifah has given love, support and dedication to all those around her, especially her two sons. I have watched her triumph from many years in abusive relationships. In spite of her hardships, Latifah graduated from college with Bachelors of Science (B.S.) and Masters of Arts (M.A.) degrees, has been an educator for the past 18 years, obtained her license as a massage therapist, is a poet and an author of two books**:** ***Suffering In Silence: Breaking the Cycle of Abuse* and *Suffering In Healing: Creating a New Cycle of Abuse*** and now her third book. She has also started an agency, ***Healthy Positive Choices,*** as a preventive tool to educate teens and young adults on the detriment of relationship abuse.

Whenever you see Latifah, she has a smile for you and positive words of wisdom. Through the pages of this book, you will feel enlightened and encouraged because she reaches within the depth of her soul through her poetry. Sit back, put your feet up and be prepared for an inspirational journey.

I proudly endorse this book of heartfelt poems. Thank you, Latifah, for being my friend, and touching my life in so many positive ways.

MOTHER DEAR

Mother Dear,
These words are
a small token of my love,
to let you know,
you are a treasured gift
from God above.
Your heart is as pure
as the feathers on a white dove.

Mother Dear,
You're a very unique woman,
one of a kind.
You are so unselfish
when it comes to your children
all the time.

Mother Dear,
You've always been there
in my time of need.
You ask no questions,
just come in record speed.

You are so special,
you're like no other.
It is a blessing
to have you as my mother.

Words can't express my
appreciation, respect and love, too
Thank you most of all, Mother Dear
for simply-
Being You!

MY FATHER

My father,
oh how I just wanted to be loved.
I needed to feel special, crying silently,
please hold me snug like a hand in a glove.

Even if for a few moments,
I hoped to have you to myself,
But that didn't happen very much.

I didn't realize at the time.
It was a beginning of my inward pain
of having a love-hate feeling for you,
that I know, you never knew.

It chipped away at my inner being
slowly, it crept up.
Before I knew it, it had erupted.

It spilled over into all my
other relationships with men.
It caused me heartache and pain.

I didn't know what the problem was then.
So, I sought help for all of my feelings deep within.

I slowly recovered. Now I'm standing up tall,
able to hold up my own wall.

Father, you know, I don't blame you anymore
I believe, you did the best you knew how to do.
Although you're not here today,
I still want to say, I hold your love
close to my heart in so many ways.

MY FIRST BORN SON

My first born son,
when I laid eyes on you,
there was a definite bond.

I remember when I held you
for the first time.
I knew you were something special
and one of a kind.

You have always danced to your own beat.
Anyone that tried to stop you,
was in for a real treat.

When you got a thought in your mind
even if it were a clear sign to stop and rewind,
there was no turning back,
you kept moving forward in record time.

You are as intelligent as they come,
thinking fast on your feet,
and not settling for any defeat.

I have seen you down,
but you always bounce back
You have a will to live and that's a fact.
You are getting your life back on track.

The positive way
in which you've turned your life around
working for your future,
and keeping your feet on solid ground
not clowning around,
makes me proud
of how your life is becoming so sound.

God has his eyes on you,
and will definitely
see you through.
May he bless your dreams
to always come true.

A MOTHER'S WORDS OF LOVE

My youngest son,
whom I feel honored to share a special bond.

I remember when you were a little boy,
you were my pride and joy.
I taught you honor and respect,
Now that you are grown, you have kept that in tact.

You're trustworthy, loyal and sincere,
especially to your friends and those you hold dear.

You're not flashy, nor are you arrogant and bold.
Instead . . . You're kind, patient and generous,
let it be told.

I love to witness how you excel
in the things you do and say.
I'm so proud of you, each and everyday.
You are a spectacular young man in so many ways.

You have a positive outlook on life.
That's what gives you that boost of energy,
to continue to strive
but always keep God, first in your life.

You have supported me through life's ups and downs,
never complaining or gesturing a negative sound,
only making me feel comfortable,
and delighted to have me around.

There are so many wonderful things about you,
I could utter, but the one thing,
I'm most proud of,
is God blessing – **ME** – to be **YOUR MOTHER!**

FINDING ME

As I sit outside looking up at the sky,
I feel the warmth of the wind blowing in my eye.
It is such a sunny day,
so illuminating as I move along my way.

As I walk on the beach, it seems
I'm just a pebble in the sand.
Sometimes it's like I get lost
out in no man's land.

What do I say?
I say, I'll keep going
and won't stop until I find my way.

What am I looking for?
I'm searching for a place where I fit in.
The comfort I feel with a close friend.

Sometimes I feel lost as I wonder around
It's like I'm searching for my soul
but it can't be found.

It's as though I've lost who I am.
I twirl and whirl around,
fall down,
then quickly stand
to face myself
who I hid from and then ran.

For a moment I forgot
that I've been blessed with a whole lot
I thank God
for opening my eyes to see
I am as wonderful as I can be.
But I had to stop, and look inside
for this precious commodity," ME"

**HAVE YOU FOUND
WHO YOU ARE?**

KINDNESS

Kindness goes a long way, today.
It doesn't cost a penny
To reach out and say,
kind words in a genuine way.

Sometimes a smile,
a simple hi, how do you do
would be sufficient to anyone, even you.

Kindness can also be passed on to others
without so much as a bother.

Once you have been touched
by kindness
you want it
to come back.
It's such a warm feeling,
you would kindly
back track.

Let kindness be a part
of your everyday life.
You shouldn't want to
leave home without it.
Because the moment
you discover
there's no kindness
among us,

you'll quickly remember
and say,

"Kindness, you're something
I want to carry with me
each and everyday".

DO YOU HAVE KINDNESS?

WHEN I LOOK IN THE MIRROR

When I look in the mirror
What do I see?
Just a reflection of the real me.

The mirror is like a façade.
It only shows the outside.
The real me, you can't see
it's inside my mind.

When I look in the mirror,
I can smile, laugh or cry.
No one knows, but me
whether it's a lie.

The outer appearance and inner mind
is what makes me who I am.
The way I feel inside
comes out in my behavior,
most of the time.

Sometimes, when I look in the mirror
and discover a frown on my face.
I'm kind of puzzled, unaware
I'm looking that way.

So I take time to search and behold,
to make the image in the mirror
congruent with what I feel in my soul.

Now, when I look in the mirror,
I know what I see, is just
a reflection making a connection
with what's going on inside of me.

HAVE YOU LOOKED IN THE MIRROR?

PERCEPTION IS YOUR REALITY

My perception, your perception,
What exactly is this thing called perception?

Perception is your reality.
What you see and how you see it, too,
Is the only thing that's real to you.

When you come into this world,
you have no perception
or even know what is real,
you're just an empty vessel
waiting to be filled.

Perception comes from your environment,
values and beliefs, too.
Only you can see through
your mind's eye,
Not someone else's point of view.

You're molded and shaped
by your environment
whether good or bad.
It's what you internalize
and then, how you perceive it
in your mind,
which causes the manifestation
in your actions, each and every time.

You build on our own perceptions,
that's the only reality you know.

No one else
can see things through your eyes.
It's all about how you view things from the inside.

Your perception and reality too,
Is the uniqueness that belongs only to YOU!

YOUR SPIRIT

Your spirit is a life long driving force,
a force that comes from the depth of your soul.

You start out with a spirit
and you can develop it at will,
you can shape it and let it work for you,
or you can let it become stagnant & still.

You choose the kind of spirit
you will have, good or bad
and direct the affect whether
happy or sad.

Your spirit is in your possession,
You shape it in a direction,
that defines your purpose and successes.

You have a unique spirit that belongs
solely to you.
You can mode, direct,
and keep it high too.

A good spirit is what keeps you going
when life seems at an all time low.
Just when you thought you couldn't
take another blow,
the spirit within pushes you and says,
GET UP and let's continue to go.

That's when you know you have a great spirit,
so strive to keep it that way.

That kind of spirit lets you know
you are alive.
Take it to motivate yourself.
Then generate it out mankind.

WHAT KIND OF SPIRIT DO YOU HAVE?

LIVE YOUR DREAMS

Live Your Dreams – Don't let them pass you by,
grab hold and follow the path
that helped create this wonderful person you are.

Live Your Dreams – It's ok to take a chance,
and ask the question, Why?
But in the meantime,
keep living your dreams,
as though tomorrow, you will die.

Live Your Dreams – Hold them near
and dear to your heart.
Have them to guide and stimulate you
right from the start.

Live Your Dreams – They can keep you
on an upward sail, motivating you
to keep moving forward,
even when you fail.

Live Your Dreams – Don't let outside influences
hold them in check,
always live life to its very best.

Live Your Dreams – Spread your wings
as you discover new things.
Know that it's up to you,
to continue to make
your dreams come true.

When it dawns into a another day,
meet the challenges head on
in a positive way.

Continue to keep your spirit alive
and pull from the best,
that's deep down
on the In-side.

ARE YOU LIVING YOUR DREAMS?

INSIDE OF ME

What's going on inside of me
is what I take time to see.
Whatever mood I'm in,
I have the say, whether I lose or win.

No one can alter the thoughts
I have within my mind,
unless I give them permission
to take control
and keep me stringing along.

I decide if I want to change,
or things to remain the same.

Each day, I have another chance
to begin again brand new and
reinvent myself, if I really want too.

This is something I should want to do,
striving to be my best and rising to great heights too.

In the midst of my continuing to be a better person inside,
I know I am tested and tried,
but I make a conscious effort
everyday to stay on the even and straight way.

I choose the path that will be soothing
to my soul. I do this by keeping
God out front and staying true to my feminine role.

Then, I know I can make it through another day,
no matter what struggles may come my way.
I have no thoughts of defeat;
fore I seek victory with every challenge I meet.

MOTHERS, LET ME SAY A FEW WORDS

Mothers, let me say a few words about how
we need to stand up and be heard.

Recognizing how we are sometimes treated
with disrespect by one another and taken for granted
just because we are mothers and do so much for others.

Mothers, let me say a few words
We have a tendency to put ourselves last
because we take on an abundance of others task.

We try to juggle a hundred things at a time
thinking we're superwomen,
and on the verge of losing our minds.

Mothers, let me say a few words
When are we going to take that much needed time for us?
Are we going to wait until it's almost time to bite the dust?

Let someone else wait on us, some of the time,
We deserve to rest our precious minds.

Mother, let me say a few words
We deserve to be treated with great respect and love,
especially when we've been given much worth from God above.

As we keep respect on our minds
let's not go back in time
or lose sight of treating our own selves' right.

Once we treat ourselves the best,
be assured someone will come along
and put it to the test.

But we must stand strong and be the example models.
If we teach people how to treat us.
Then respect is sure to follow.

PHENOMENAL WOMAN

Phenomenal woman-that's who I am
During childhood, I had to be strong-
although I felt so all alone.

Life was filled with twist and turns
along the way, but I was determined
not to be defeated on any given day.
Phenomenal woman-that's who I am

As a child,
I tried to keep it together
without knowing what to expect,
just knowing my life was a wreck.

My mom and dad did the best
they could
like parents should,
but it wasn't enough like I hoped it would.

It's funny how they thought most of my life
that I was all right.
Little did they know,
in reality, most of the time,
I was putting on a good show.
Phenomenal woman-that's who I am.

I kept putting one foot in front of the other,
like I knew I had too.
I didn't know where I was going
discreetly following any way the wind was blowing.

You see, I was and still am a fighter, a soldier and more.
I don't give up easily; I keep bucking
and standing strong like a steel door.
Phenomenal woman-that's who I am

There were times when
I felt I wouldn't make it thru another day,
but with the strength of God,
he kept pushing me along the right way.
He helped me keep it together during childhood
but even more so today.
Phenomenal woman-that's who I am

Each challenge was a dose of reality for me,
but I kept looking for the silver lining
in the cloud so I could clearly see.
What is it – I'm supposed to be?

It looks like since I was going through such a battle,
maybe I'm here to rattle and detour
others from repeating my travel,
while teaching self-love,
something that really matters.

Perhaps I'm here to help pull off the phony masks,
while revealing the real person, something
that wasn't done in the past,

Then without the mask, others can stand tall,
loving who they are – feeling no defeat at all.
Taking on life's task – not hiding behind the mask.
Saying "Ah, I can stand strong,
look at the model that's been behind me all along".
Then I will know all I went through wasn't in vein,
There was a cause bigger than I could ever name.

I stand before you today to say,
take time to pray
Then pay attention to the things that stand in your way.
Work to be a better person each and everyday.
Teach people how to treat you every step of the way.

Know that each one of us is unique within
and have the staying power to handle
trials and tribulations down to the very end.
Phenomenal woman-that's who I am

FAILURE IS NOT FAILURE UNTIL . . .

Failure is not failure until . . .
You give up before you get started,
wondering why you feel so disheartened.

Failure in not failure until . . .
You fall and don't get up.
That's when the struggle really gets tough.

Failure is not failure until . . .
You allow others to run your life,
giving up on yourself without so much as a try.

Failure is not failure until . . .
You stop reaching for your goals.
Not listening to your mind or searching for that open road.

Failure is not failure until . . .
You have no real purpose in life
giving up the struggle to live and strive.

Failure is not failure until . . .
You give up on your dreams,
and desire for life not even caring about anything in sight.

Failure is not failure until . . .
You refuse to stand up for what you believe in.
Don't you know, if you don't stand for something, you will fall for any darn thing.

Failure is not failure until . . .
You can't face yourself each day knowing
you need to believe in you and the things you do and say.

If you want failure to be something of the past,
face each day with a renewed spirit
and continuous commitment to help you on your way.

Once you have an understanding of what failure truly is,
then failure is something you have no need to bother
yourself with Ever – Again.

GOD GRANT US SERENITY

God grant us serenity-
Fore times like these
demand strong mind, true faith
and ready hands
in order to move across this land
before we all explode like mines.

God grant us serenity-
Fore we must constantly be
on guard against discouragement and doubts,
but with the help of God,
we are casting the negativity right on out.

God grant us serenity-
Fore our victories are great but few.
It matters no how hard we strive
each day our hope is renewed.

God grant us serenity
Fore our goals are sometimes
stiffened by circumstances,
our plans hung up by narrow minds.

We've had to crawl, climb and swim fighting
for every stubborn yard but we have
kept in fighting trim.
God Grant Us Serenity to the end!

CREATION

When you look into creation,
there is so much power and beauty
in what God can do.

In his infinite wisdom,
he shows how creation
is in an orderly fashion too.

When day comes night
gets out of the way
it's in the order
that God so vividly displays.

Creation is an excellent example
of how human beings
should live their lives,
a continuous stride
all the time not just once in a while.

The sun comes out in the day
and the moon at night.
Each does its job accordingly
and gets out of sight.

In creation, God speaks to us
so very loud and clear.
The lessons we think are far away
are really quite near.

If we would just take time and listen,
creation will tell us what we need to know.

It's guaranteed that the messages revealed
will amaze our life so,
We'll have a new fond
respect for creation, everywhere we go

PRAYER

Prayer is the key
to a peaceful life within.
Through prayer, all things are possible,
because God showers
his blessings to the end.

God answers all prayers
in his own time
not when we want a quick response
or in a serious bind.

While in prayer,
we must ask God to keep us on
the straight
and narrow path.

It's so important as we go through
life's various tasks.

Prayer is so refreshing
to the mind, body and soul.
It makes believers feel so very whole.

Let's keep prayer alive in our lives at all times.
One of the many benefits is a peace of mind.

THE BELIEVERS

The believers are mighty strong-willed human beings.
They dedicate their whole lives to God,
and go on blind faith without seeing.

The believers are very different you see.
The stages of their spiritual development
reaches the highest it could ever be.

The believers are to be commented
on their unselfish dedication to God on high.
They strive to reach peak performance
day and night without so much as a sigh.

They ask God to use them in a way
that will serve him best.
They trust his wisdom completely
to put them through any test.

The believers try to be the best role models
for all people to see.
They stand up for the this truth
like dedicated soldiers should always be.

The believers have a continuous glowing bright light.
Their model examples will peak
the curiosity of people
who are searching and
wanting to live their lives right.

OUR BLACK BROTHERS STRUGGLE

Our black brothers, oh, how you all have had to struggle,
to keep your dignity, strong mind and pride.
You all have had to keep the faith in very hard times,
so you could move across this land and not explode like mines.

Our black brothers, you've had to constantly be on guard
against discouragements and doubt.
The reason you all have made it this far,
is God blessing you to cast the negatively on out.

Our black brothers, the struggle is ongoing,
but you must not stop, don't you all know,
when black men unite, they will be on top.

Our black brothers, you've had to crawl,
climb and swim to keep in tact what you have built.
BUT – you all have kept in fighting trim,
and there is a deep seeded will in you all to continue to live.

Our black brothers, sometimes you forget
we need your backbone to keep our families strong.

You must always keep your spirit alive.
We black sisters need you by our sides.
We support, respect and salute you too.
Fore you all are our heroes through and through.

Sometimes frustration seems to warp your wills,
but keep your heads up, our black brothers,
Fore you are all certainly
Undefeated still!!

IN WAITING

Waiting by the phone for that call,
that call that never came at all.

Wanting to feel special to someone
to connect and have a bond.

Waiting for love and the pursuit of happiness,
not knowing what it really looks like,
just hoping to feel the bliss

Waiting as the ups go down
never sure if I will find love
or whether I will recognize it
if it ever came around.

Waiting to see if this is the right man this time,
wanting to be in love maybe this one will be mine.

Sometimes I feel as though I have two left feet,
going back and forth never getting anywhere,
just falling on defeat.

I keep waiting for the love that can only be found,
found within me by making my self-love sound.

Once I connect to the love inside of me,
Confidence will shine for all to see.
I'll bring out the real beauty within me.

The waiting will be over as well as defeat,
because self-love is the sustaining force behind
building and making my life complete.
ARE YOU IN WAITING?

THAT ILLUSION OF BEING BLACK

We were once in physical slavery against our will.
We're now physically free, but in chains still
This time, the chains are on our minds in many ways.
There's a subtle message given out each and everyday.

The message is, we're black in a white man's world, you see.
Playing by their rules,
so they can keep us right where they think we ought to be.
That Illusion of Being Black

In an indirect way, they let us know,
we are at their mercy in more ways than we think so.
It's evident in the way we fight among each other, blow by blow,
like we're in a circus show . . .
Caught up, so we don't use our minds to grow.

It's all a part of a plot,
to keep the control and our minds locked.

When we integrated into the melting pot,
we were sucked in, and that put us,
at their mercy, in the lion's den.
That Illusion of Being Black

When we bought into this myth,
the control began, we weren't aware
we were too busy,
trying to be just like them.

We're so confused, sometimes,
we don't know, if we're coming or going.

Don't you see,
it's been designed that way.
It's a direct result of the conditioning they hope,
will always stay.

Do you realize,
we've been taught to hate who we are.
We think, if we're light, bright or damn near white,
we are all right.
That Illusion of Being Black

When we have our hair fried, dyed,
and laid to the side,
to get rid of our so called nappy hair,
then, we think, we have truly arrived.

Nothing could be further from the truth.
We've been programmed to think,
when we look in the mirror and see our big lips,
wide noses and hair curled up tight we aren't accepted,
nor do we feel right.
That Illusion of Being Black

They have made natural
seem unnatural
by turning things inside out,
quietly projecting self-hate . . .
We fail to see all of this,
right in our face.

God made us who we are, and he creates no mess.
We are paying the price
for allowing this scheme
to take over so much or our life.
But we can rise above it and make it right.

We need to wake up,
become more aware,
pay closer attention to what is being said and done,
and not burying our heads, acting as though nothing is wrong.

Let's get out-of-that Illusion of being black,
examine the reality-
redirect our minds, and then begin – to take – OUR Lives Back!
Are you Living that Illusion of Being Black?

A BETTER ME

When the lights went out
and the room was still
I was alone with myself
For me, that was a big deal.

In the past, I felt being alone
was a bad thing.
Now I see, I needed time to develop me.

When I take time
to quiet my soul,
I can rejuvenate my spirit,
become whole, in the midst of displaying
my feminine role.

I keep a positive attitude on board
trusting that my Lord,
will guide and keep me moving forward.

When I make a choice
I trust what I feel within
not giving anyone permission to take me
on a whim perhaps putting me
out on a limb.

As each day goes by,
I'm becoming a better person
through and through all because
my Lord is blessing me
with the strength to endure.
Fore each day, I am reassured.

WHY DO I FEEL ALIENATED

Why do I feel alienated in a world full of people
with whom I feel no real connection.

I have tried to reach out, but it's as though
no one is there.
It's like searching around in the dark.
Everywhere I look, I hear voices, but I don't see a soul.
Why do I feel alienated?

Even when people are around,
I get the same . . . effect.
I stand alone and invisible,
Why do I feel alienated?

People don't know who I am.
They won't take time to understand,
or even give a damn.
Why do I feel alienated?

When I'm out in the society,
I begin to look around.
I search for some connection,
but none can be found.
I sneak a peak around the corner,
and try to make all kinds of sounds.
so anyone will pay attention to me,
but all I get is a whole lot of nothing but frowns.
Am I just a clown?
Why do I feel alienated?

Maybe, I'm alienated because of the way I see myself inside.
After all, it's all about my own state of mind!
Do you feel Alienated?

THE STRANGER WITHIN

I talk to you everyday,
but I really don't know who you are.
I rationalize the way I want you to be,
I even put on a façade.

I want to be accepted by people on the outside,
but I must realize
It's what I think of me that really matters.
I do things and say, that's just the way I am.
without examining why I say it in that way.
I don't take time to listen to the stranger within.
I don't know,
nor do I identify what makes me who I am.
I fail to understand what's being dictated to me
from the stranger within.

I put blinders on so I can't see the reality of me.
I think I'm on top of my game,
but I don't know a damn thing.
I allow others to come in,
shape and mold my behavior,
and I'm not even aware
of what's happening to me.

I think I'm in control, but all along,
I'm the one who is being played on.

I hide behind laughter, (ha, ha)
when I really want to cry.
I don't know why I feel this way.
Sometimes I just want to die.

These feelings are scary.
I don't understand what's happening to me,
But the stranger within cries out to
Stop . . . and take a look inside myself to see.

I'm so busy trying to impress,
putting on an act that I don't see,
I'm the one being laughed at.

I need to take the time to examine my mind,
thoughts and actions,
to understand why I react in the ways that I do.

I need to internalize on the inside,
Stop being what others have dictated
who I should be and
start focusing in on the real me.

The stranger within only wants me
to come into my true being,
listening to what my voice says on the inside
tuning the loud noise on the outside
realizing, I'm the one in control of my mind.

I will know when the real me has began
because I will have become one with
the stranger within
Are you connected to the stranger within?

WEARING A MASK

Are you wearing a mask?
Parading around town, unaware
your life is upside down,
so busy playing around
acting foolish like a clown
wanting to be in
with the in crowd.

Underneath the mask,
there's nothing
but a face full of frowns,
and no substance to be found.

This has been
the pretend you for so long,
you wouldn't know the real you
if you came along.

Everyday, you put on your mask
going about your daily tasks,
afraid to say what's really
on your mind
hiding behind the mask.

It's just a matter of time
before someone sees two of you
because the frustration
will eventually seep through.
Then, someone will ask,
"What's up with you?"

You'll act as though
nothing is wrong.
All along, wearing two faces
singing opposite songs.

Which one is really you?
I guess it will depend on
what mood comes through.

As you go through life like this,
things continue
to unravel with a twist.
Fear is behind all of these risks.
Wearing a mask is like
putting salt on an open wound.

It will hurt badly, and
healing won't be in sight soon.
Take off the mask.
show who you really are.
Stop hiding behind the truth.
Let the real you shine through.
You might discover,
you like who you are, too.
Are You Wearing A Mask?

SISTAHS

We have always been sistahs
in this world, don't you know
from the beginning of time,
we have struggled
to beat the negative light
that has labeled us so.

It doesn't matter
about our race, creed or color,
we are women,
with a common love
for each other.

The way in which
we continue to survive
is to keep God alive in our lives
having a unified mind
standing side by side.

There is strength in numbers,
I know you sistahs are aware.
Let's not tear each other down
by our jealousy and snares.

We come out better when we stick together
especially when our minds are focused
so our bond won't be broken.

Sistahs we need to realize,
we're not going to always
see eye to eye in our endeavors,
but we must respect the uniqueness
each one brings to the table.

Sistahs, we need each other.
We need to be real, feel safe
trust and have each other backs
especially during tough times,
because we're all we've got.

Sistahs, sistahs, let's wake up
be wise and realize,
we need each other in our lives
by our side.
The harder we strive
to stay together,
the longer
we will survive.
Sistah's, Let's stick together!

FREE TO BE ME!

I am free to be me
in my life
where it counts, you see.

Not letting someone dictate
how I should be.

Being able to think for myself
trusting what I feel
and know it to be real,
reaching within my soul
taking a chance and being bold
FREE TO BE ME

Walking tall, feeling no defeat at all
breaking down negativity
as if it were a brick wall.
FREE TO BE ME

Expressing myself and not being scared
that someone may not like what I said.
Lifting my head up and continuing to be strong.
Knowing with God out front I can't go wrong.
FREE TO BE ME

Letting the world know
I am steady moving on my way.
I will not be silenced
because I have something to say.
Look at me, can't you see?
I am ***FREE – TO BE ME***

TRUE LOVE

True Love touches the depth of your soul.
It's like having a treasure to behold.

True Love is such a gift to you and me.
It touches the heart in places only
that one special person can see.

True Love can be such a pleasure and delight.
It makes you feel fortunate
to have that person in your life.

True love gives you the strength
to hold up your end.
It makes you want to stick with someone
through thick and thin.

True Love can bring joy into your life everyday.
It's something you'll want to keep that way.
Don't take it for granted because it may be gone one day.

True Love gives you happiness in a variety of ways.
The feelings warm your heart
and stays fresh in your mind throughout the day.

When true love is present
you have a secure feeling within,
and pray your love will be presence
right down to the end.

Hold true love close to your heart,
through and through, keep nurturing it everyday
just like it was brand new.
Do You Have True Love?

WHAT IS RESPECT?

Respect is something that must be earned.
Before it can be genuinely given out,
one must weigh their concerns.

Concerns from how one treats another
not with arrogance
or by stepping on their sister or brother,
demanding something
that should be natural in coming.

Some people expect respect,
because they feel they are the best, above the rest.
Just because one has status and prestige
doesn't give them a ticket for respect
thinking they're all that.

They're in for a rude awakening.
The respect will be unreal, not from the heart,
something artificial on the surface maybe,
an attitude with a cold chill.

When respect is given from within,
It's presence is felt, because it's the real thing.

How respect is defined
is unique to one's own perception.
Most people look for attitude,
dedication and character too.
That helps determine
the level of respect from one's own point of view.

Respect is a real touchy thing.
Before you give it, take time to examine
the true character of the HUMAN BEING.
Are you Worthy of Respect?

LOOK AT ME!

Look at me, Look at me. Can't you see
I am the creation of Almighty God on high.
I'm not perfect, oh no, not by far.

Look at how I've been blessed
with a uniqueness that belongs only to me.
I am a Nubian Queen, can't you see?
Look at Me! Look at Me!

My beauty lies within my soul,
I know that's the essence of me,
let it be told. I'm not arrogant, nor am I ex-ceed-ingly bold,
because I humble myself
to my creator first and foremost.

I'm nothing without my God guiding me along.
I know with him anything is possible and not much will go wrong.
What really matters is serving my God,
then how I treat me, which transfers on to mankind.

Life in this world can make me believe
it's all that, what an illusion, because I will be called back,
to answer for the foolishness
I let take over my life. I will be accountable,
and I know that to be right.

As long as I stay on the straight and narrow path,
I will remain sane, but without protection
is a guarantee of pain.

Pain from unnecessary struggle
from the insanity of society. The hustle and bustle of life
makes me think twice. Think twice about where I'm headed,
examine my actions, all my decisions,
to make sure I have a spiritual connection.
Look at Me, Can't you See, God has Truly Blessed Me!

ATTITUDE

Attitude is everything, you see.
How you construct it,
is the way the outcome will be.

Your attitude will definitely display,
what's in your heart,
by the words you say.
How you view it,
is how you will react to it.

Sometime when things
seem overwhelming to you,
you might have the tendency
to form a negative attitude
all the way through.

To construct the best attitude
in any given situation,
stop, make a decision
based on a positive thought
and put that on top.
It's better in the long run
after it's all said and done.

It will cause you less stress
and will put you
mentally above the rest.

The rest of those people
who let negative attitudes
dominate their thoughts.

They don't grow,
they just stand still
and let that negativity guide
the way in which
they will live.
Don't let this be you, take control.
You know what to do.
Think about your reactions
and attitudes too.

When you respond to things,
remember to add a positive ring.
It will help you grow into a better
Human Being.
How is your attitude?

DEPRESSION DOESN'T LIVE HERE ANYMORE

I remember a time when depression had taken over my body and mind.

It was like a familiar song. It played every time something went wrong.
I would give into it and find myself way, way down to the ground.

It would fester in me, my soul would be so disturbed, you see.
One thing I didn't realize, I was on my way to suicide.
When you would look at me, you'd think I had it together.
Inside, it was far worse than anyone could image.

I had to take a good look at depression.
It was taking over my life's expression.
I didn't feel good about me, so I begin to look on the inside to see.

Once I discovered, I was the one who really mattered,
I began to unravel all those feelings with a battle.
Depression doesn't live here anymore.

I soon begin to explore all the interesting things that lie within.
It was like I was on stage with stardom being my gauge.
What a fascinating discovery of a self so well put together.
Depression doesn't live here anymore.

I got to know more about me from the inside.
It took time, and I'm still finding out
new things about myself each day.
I take time to find out who I am in a variety of ways.

Depression wants to visit and stay a day or so.
But each time it starts to linger around,
I quickly show it out the door,
because depression doesn't live here anymore
and that's for Sure!

LIFE FOR ME AIN'T BEEN NO GOLDEN STAIR

Life for me ain't been no golden stair.
There's been cracks, tacks, and a whole lot of snares.

I've had to be tough,
in order to take a lot of stuff.

Many times I wanted to give up, and quit,
but I knew I had a purpose,
that kept me strong through all the head trips.

Life for me ain't been no golden stair.
I'd had to stay strong, hold up my head
and sometimes even stand alone.

I came through an abusive marriage
where I was truly scared.

I was hit, kicked and oppressed
and went through a lot of mess.

I finally got enough courage to leave.
I said-No More – of this distress.

I made it through those terrible days
and I'm here to say,
Although life for me ain't been no golden stair,
Look at how far God has brought me,
with all I've had to bear.

I'm living proof,
God will always be near.
But you have to reach out and
trust that he'll always be there.

TOUGH TIMES

Tough times, tough times, what can I say?
When they come, they seem to want to stay,
lingering around, like they don't want to go away.
They make you cringe, even double over with a bend.

Know that everyone falls
on tough times every now and then.
That's when you need a friend to be there,
to see you through the end.

But, you must be the one to weather the storm.
In the midst of it, you could transform.
You could even come out stronger.
There are times you might have to endure a little longer.
But you must not quit, no matter how hard it gets.
The clouds may be heavy along the way
Maybe blind your sight for days.

But know the clouds will soon dissipate.
Things will work out, sometimes in different ways.
Don't let tough times get you down.
They'll only defeat you, if you let them hang around.
Don't let them take away your fight.
Keep the faith alive
and know that tough times are just a part of life.

WHY ME?

"Why Me", "Why Me",
is what I said when things went wrong
and I felt weak and wasn't very strong.
Did I think, I could go through life
with everything always going right?

I needed to understand,
that I would be tried and tested
with my goods and personal self.

Sometimes the tests will come fast,
sometimes they'll be slow,
but I must know it's part of life,
and I can ease the blow.

Ease the blow by living a righteous life,
putting God first is safe, I must say.
Then I'm less likely to go astray.

When I live right,
it helps to keep those negative thoughts
out of mind and sight.

I need to stay focused,
so my spirit wouldn't be broken.
I look at
how far I've come, not dwelling
on the negative things I've done.

Each day is an opportunity
for me to begin
again brand new.

Just as I'm striving and climbing further
"Why me" will come back to bother,
with all the negative groans,
trying to suck me in
to listen to the moans.

"Why me" really doesn't belong
and has no where to roam.

At one time, I needed "Why me"
as a crutch to lean on, that need is gone.
I have become strong,
I can stand on my own.
I'm steadily moving right along.

SELF LOVE

When self love is truly there,
you'll feel it through and through.
It will be the spirit that dwells inside of you.

When self love is truly within
You'll know happiness
It will be part of your being.
When self love is truly there
It's like a ray of hope in the air.

When you walk in the room,
confidence will shine,
you'll be rare, like a fine wine.
No need to say a word
It will be in your smile,
on your face,
you'll glide with such grace.
When self love is truly there
you'll have self-respect
which commands
to be treated the best.

When someone does otherwise
you will quickly rise
politely excuse yourself
this is treatment you won't accept.

When self-love is truly there
Self-esteem will be the best
because you won't settle
for anything less.

How do you show your Self-Love?

I AM THE ONE

I held you up when you could no longer stand.
I was there to wipe your tears as they flowed like
a fountain that overran.

I gave you hope when you thought there
was none, that hope is now faith
that shines like a beaming sun.

I've soothed your soul when the burden was too much.
I reached out and lifted you up with my touch.

I've watched over you, while you grew into the woman you are today.
Sometimes I let you stumble, but guided you along the way.

I gave you courage and strengthened you within.
I kept you on the straight way even when you strayed now and then.

I am your Merciful Redeemer, who has given
you life. Remember to keep me in front
of everything, as you continue to strive.

I'm always there and solid as a board.
But it's up to you to call on me,
I'm unchangeable, fore I am your **Lord**.

THE BEST IS YET TO COME

The best is yet to come.
You have just begun,
a journey into your mind
to pull out those talents
you thought you left behind.

Challenge yourself,
to reach your goals, and to know
you are the head master
of your show.
The Best is Yet to Come.

Examine where you're headed
and have a structured plan
as you move full force
in record speed
across this land.
The Best is Yet to Come.

Reach your highest level
rise to the top,
the sky's the limit
no matter how tough
you must not stop
The Best is Yet to Come.

Trust yourself,
to test your limits
develop your inner strength
exercise your mental
muscles and practice your wit.
The Best is Yet to Come.

You can do it.
believe in yourself.
you're your #1 fan.
continue to work
your lifelong plan.
The Best is Yet to Come.

Don't you know,
everything you need
is right in the palms of your hands.
The Best is Yet to Come.

It's up to you
to carry it through,
keep it going
while you're growing
and when everything is done,
you will have worked it
and think
you have truly won.
But remember,
The Best is STILL, Yet to Come

THE REAL YOU

To discover the real you,
it takes reaching within your soul,
to understand what really motivates
your mind to go.

Not the make believe,
the fake things that are hollow
at the end of a scene.

A scene in which you play a pretend star
knowing that's not who you really are.
It's too much resistance and imbalance
going against your very soul.

When you take a good look, you'll see
all that drama is not what it's cracked up to be.

The real you listens to what is being said.
staying in tune with your inner moods,
keeping harmony, balance and inner peace.

Inner peace will keep you
conscious of your duty to self,

and help stabilize your mind
so no one can come in
and break you down
especially when you're
standing on solid ground.

When you come into a room
no need to say a word.
your confidence will shine
like a piecing light,
ever so bright, in your eyes
on your face, the way you move
it's ever so smooth
in everything you do.
No pretending that's the real you.

When you know the real you,
you understand,
what's portrayed on the outside
is a direct reflection
of how you think
and in what direction.

When certain problems keep
repeating in your live,
take time to examine, ask the question, why?
seek the answer; this could be the very thing
that helps to mend your broken wing.
Sometimes pain from problems
seem hard to face
many times you want to bow out of the race.
Flip the script,
so you won't be part of the trip.

That's when you – STOP – take a good look
seek the truth, bring all those thoughts together
so you will become a better person
in the midst of the struggle.

Take a chance, make a stance
come into the knowledge of self
beyond a glance.

Its all worth it to know,
understand and comprehend
the Real You!
Do You Know the Real You?

A HEALTHY SELF-ESTEEM

Having a healthy self-esteem
is something that will make you gleam
the feeling within motivates you to win.

Having a healthy self-esteem
brings you joy and delight.
You let no one come in
and steal your bright light.

There's a non stopping spirit
that comes from the inside out
it's enlightening, without a doubt.

Having a healthy self-esteem
allows you to be the best.
Even when you're put through a test,
you never settle for less.

If you fall, or run into a brick wall keep getting up,
eventually you'll stand tall.

When you have a healthy self-esteem,
confidence, definitely rings,
people notice the radiant beam.

These are a few positive things,
a healthy self-esteem brings.
Do You Have a Healthy Self-Esteem?

EXISTENCE

Have you ever given it a moment's thought,
why God brought our very existence about?

We were put here to serve him
in so many ways.
Some of us take our existence
for granted everyday.

We must wake up,
take time to be grateful
for what God
has given us on this earth.

If we weren't a special creation,
He wouldn't have allowed
our mothers to give us birth.

Walking, talking, breathing and seeing
are just a few of the precious gifts
God has blessed us with.
If we think it's all for nothing,
we're living a myth.

God creates everything with a purpose.
Look at how everything in creation
is so structured.

When day comes, night moves out of the way.
It's in the order, God so vividly displays.

Let's take a closer look at our existence,
and keep our eyes open so we can see,
that we need to be thankful
for who God has blessed us to be.

YOU CAN BE THE STAR OF YOUR SHOW

If you want
to be the star of your show,
you have to shine,
being genuine all the time.

Not sitting on the sidelines,
waiting for
someone else to pull you through,
like a puppet,
being told what to do,
not using your mind.
Do you want this to be you?

You can be the star of your show,
but you have
to be real with yourself first.
Stop trying
to be something you're not,
too afraid to call your own shots.

Come clean
with how you really feel.
Stand up
for what you believe to be real.
Be a person of truth,
love yourself inside first,
through and through.
It all starts inside of You.

POSITIVE ATTITUDE SEEDS

Positive attitude seeds
are something we all need.
When it comes to keeping our spirit renewed,
we all need the right attitude.
Not just on the surface,
but all the way through.

Plant a positive seed
everywhere you go.
You may need to count on it
when you're feeling kind of low.

Sometimes a negative attitude seed
can be planted
without your permission.
It may creep in
and begin to take over your being.

When you see
that negative attitude seed
begin to show,
immediately pull it out,
so it won't continue to grow.

Then you can stand back and see
just how beautiful and inspiring
a positive attitude seed can be.

THE HUMAN BEING

God has created the human being in such rare
and unique form.

Just think of that tiny blood clot of flesh
in the womb waiting to be born.

It's so amazing how the human being is
so meticulously put together.

In the beginning stage of life, it didn't weigh
much more than a feather.

Then the human being was clothed
with a head, arms, fingers and legs.
Pushing to be developed
full force ahead.

God creates these
miraculous human beings
with planted tiny seeds

From the initial stage of the
human being
it was made in God's image
and that's
the Highest Form, indeed.

NOTES

NOTES

NOTES

LaVergne, TN USA
10 February 2010
172580LV00004B/25/P